A Kid's Guide to Drawing the Countries of the World™

How to Draw
Egypt's
Sights and Symbols

Betsy Dru Tecco

The Rosen Publishing Group's
PowerKids Press™
New York

To my sweet Elise for being patient...and sleeping

Published in 2004 by The Rosen Publishing Group, Inc.
29 East 21st Street, New York, NY 10010

First Edition

Editor: Frances E. Ruffin
Book Design: Kim Sonsky
Layout Design: Maria E. Melendez

Illustration Credits: Inside and cover by Emily Muschinske
Photo Credits: Cover and title page (hand) by Arlan Dean; cover, pp. 22 (step pyramid), 26 © Sandro Vannini/CORBIS; p. 5 © Roger Ressmeyer/CORBIS; pp. 6, 10 © Richard T. Nowitz/CORBIS; p. 9 © Roger Wood/CORBIS; pp. 12, 13 courtesy of Hoda Murad; p. 18 © Dave Bartfuff/CORBIS; p. 20 © Hanan Isachar/CORBIS; p. 24 © Ian McKinnell/Getty Images; p. 28 © Archivo Iconografico, S.A./CORBIS; p. 30 © Carmen Redondo/CORBIS; p. 32 © Julia Waterlow, Eye Ubiquitous/CORBIS; p. 34 © Bettmann/CORBIS; p. 36 © Michael Nicholson/CORBIS; p. 38 © Angelo Hornak/CORBIS; p. 40 © Arte & Immagini srl/CORBIS; p. 42 © Lloyd Cluff/CORBIS.

Tecco, Betsy Dru.
How to draw Egypt's sights and symbols / Betsy Dru Tecco.
    p. cm.— (A kid's guide to drawing the countries of the world)
Summary: Presents step-by-step directions for drawing the national flag, an Arabian camel, a pyramid, and other sights and symbols of Egypt.
Includes bibliographical references and index.
  ISBN 0-8239-6682-8 (lib. bdg.)
1. Egypt—In art—Juvenile literature. 2. Drawing—Technique—Juvenile literature. 3. Egypt—Juvenile literature. [1. Egypt—In art. 2. Drawing—Technique.] I. Title. II. Series.
  NC825.E38 T43 2004
  743'.93662—dc21
                                                                2002013499

Manufactured in the United States of America

Contents

Let's Draw Egypt

The country of Egypt is one of the world's oldest civilizations. This ancient land was home to the first society to form a national government. That was about 5,000 years ago. Menes, an Egyptian leader, became Egypt's first king in 3100 B.C. He joined the people of Upper Egypt in the south and Lower Egypt in the north to form one country.

Later Egyptian kings were called pharaohs. Some had huge stone pyramids built for their burial sites. The Great Pyramid of Giza was completed around 2580 B.C. for King Khufu. Taller than a 40-story building, it is the world's largest pyramid. It is believed that at least 20,000 workers spent 20 years building the pyramid. They used more than two million blocks of stone. Each stone weighed between 2 and 15 tons (1.8–13.6 t). Near the pyramid is the famous Sphinx. This stone structure is 240 feet (73.2 m) long and 66 feet (20.1 m) high. No one knows who built the Sphinx, or why this stone statue of a lion with the head of a king was created.

Ancient Egyptians were masters of construction and

These three pyramids in Giza, Egypt, are among the most famous structures in the world. They include the Great Pyramid, which is the oldest, built in 2580 B.C., and the Pyramids of Khafre and Menkaure.

This photograph shows the Great Sphinx, which is lit up, and the Pyramid of Khafre. Both are located at Giza, Egypt. Khafre was the son of King Khufu, who built the Great Pyramid, which is nearby.

science long before the Greeks and the Romans. While other people were stuck in the Stone Age, the Egyptians invented a calendar. They invented a way to write with pictures, known as hieroglyphics. They even made paper using a plant called papyrus.

At different times in history, people from other nations conquered Egypt. However, Egypt has had many powerful leaders. One of Egypt's most famous rulers was Cleopatra VII. She was the daughter of Ptolemy XII, a Greek army officer who conquered Egypt and became its ruler. In 69 B.C., Cleopatra became Egypt's queen at the age of 18. After her reign ended in 31 B.C., Egypt became part of the Roman Empire. By the fourth century, Christianity was Egypt's official religion. Until this time, Egyptians had believed in many gods. They believed the pharaohs were gods, too. Today Copts, or Egyptian Christians, make up about 10 percent of the population. Saint Catherine's Monastery, built at Mount Sinai in A.D. 530, is still home to Coptic monks.

After the Romans, Arab Muslims ruled Egypt for hundreds of years. Egypt adopted the Arabic language as well as the Muslim faith of Islam, which is practiced by 90 percent of Egyptians. In this book, you will read about some of Egypt's most famous sights and symbols. You will need the following supplies to draw Egypt's one-of-a-kind treasures:

- A sketch pad
- An eraser
- A number 2 pencil
- A pencil sharpener

These are some of the shapes and drawing terms you need to know to draw Egypt's sights and symbols:

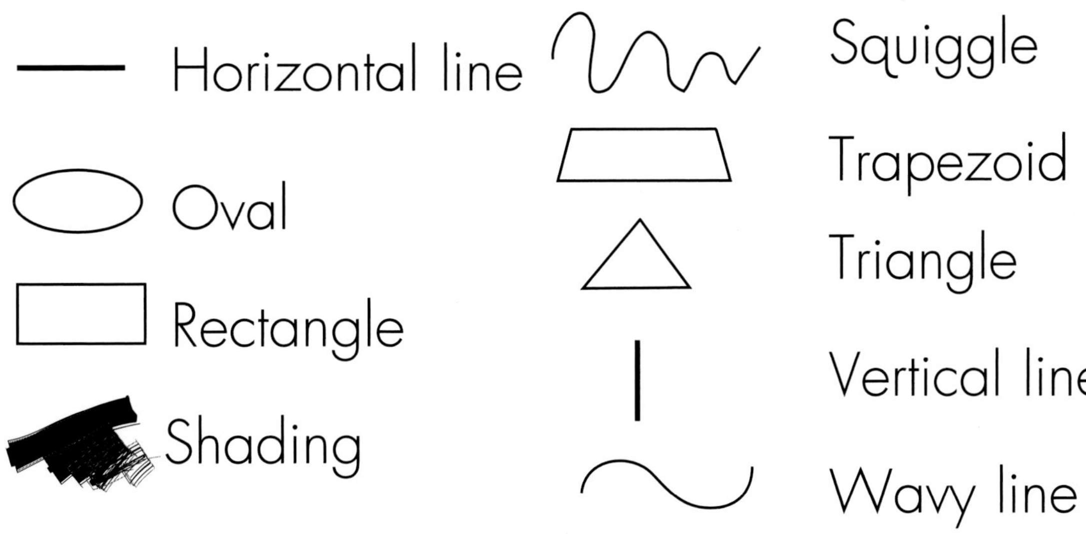

—— Horizontal line

Oval

Rectangle

Shading

Squiggle

Trapezoid

Triangle

| Vertical line

Wavy line

More About Egypt

Great Britain occupied Egypt in 1882. A revolution in 1952 ended decades of British rule. It also ended the Egyptian monarchy. Egypt's government became a republic in 1953, led by a president and a prime minister. Today the country is a leader among Arab nations. In 1979, Egypt became the first Arab country to sign a peace agreement with Israel. The historic plan was signed by Egyptian president Anwar el-Sadat and Israeli prime minister Menachem Begin. It ended 30 years of war between the two countries.

The majority of Egyptians are descended from either the ancient Egyptians or from the Arabs. Nubians, a small group of Egyptians, have lived for centuries in southern Egypt. The bedouin people make up another group in Egypt. They mostly roam the desert with their large families and their animals. Some bedouins have settled in oases and seacoast villages.

Half of Egypt's nearly 65 million people live in its cities. The capital, Cairo, is the largest city in the Arab world. The next three major Egyptian cities are

Saint Catherine's Monastery is located at the foot of Mount Sinai. The monastery was built on the place where it is believed that Moses of the Bible's Old Testament saw a burning bush as a sign from God. Mount Sinai is also the location where Moses is said to have received the Ten Commandments.

Alexandria, Al-Jizah, and Shubra al-Khaymah. Outdoor bazaars and village markets called souks are busy, noisy places. People sell everything from spices to camels. Customers bargain for the best price. They try to pay as little as possible.

About 40 percent of Egyptians are farmers who work in fields or who herd flocks of sheep and goats. Many use old-fashioned methods. Cows and oxen pull a simple plow. Some Egyptians travel by donkey or camel. Egypt's main crops are cotton, rice, and corn. Egypt has a major textile industry. It is the world's leading producer of quality cotton. Oil and natural gas are two of Egypt's biggest natural resources. Another large source of income is the Suez Canal. Every day, ships from around the world must pay to pass through the canal.

While Egypt continues to grow as a modern society, its people live surrounded by its great past. The children play soccer, their favorite sport, in the shadows of monuments that have survived for thousands of years.

Egyptians gather daily at this camel market in Imbabah, near Cairo, to sell and buy camels. Most of the camels are brought there from the country of Libya by camel dealers.

The Artist Hoda Mourad

Hoda Mourad

Artist Hoda Mourad was born in Cairo, Egypt, in 1944. Her interest in drawing began when she was a little girl, just learning to hold a crayon or pencil. Her mother noticed that Hoda had a talent for art. By the age of six, Hoda was taking lessons from a private art teacher.

She enjoyed drawing and painting, but it wasn't until she was married and the mother of two sons that Mourad continued her art studies. She graduated from the Faculty of Arts at Cairo University in 1969, and began to show her artwork at exhibitions. First, she exhibited her paintings throughout Egypt. Since then her work has been on display in Egyptian embassies around the world, including in the countries of Kuwait and England, and in the cities of Madrid, Spain, Vienna, Austria, and Paris, France.

Mourad is an impressionist artist, which means she paints in a style of art known as impressionism. She studied the work of Claude Monet, the famous French

12

impressionist who was the first artist to show how sunlight can change the way an object looks. Like Monet and other impressionist artists, Mourad uses drawing knives, thick paints, and bright colors to create her works of art.

Mourad, married to a doctor whose work took the family to Nigeria and Kuwait, now lives in Cairo, the capital city of her home country of Egypt. She also has a farm nearby and it is there that Mourad does most of her work. Her favorite subjects to paint are the crowded markets of old Cairo and the old sailboats that in her paintings appear to dance in the sea. She also likes to paint flowers.

Going to the Market (Old Cairo) is an oil-on-canvas painting that Hoda Mourad created in the year 2000. It is a typical scene of an outdoor village market in the older section of Cairo, Egypt.

Map of Egypt

EGYPT

Map of the Continent of Africa

Egypt is located on the continent of Africa, except for Egypt's Sinai Peninsula, which lies in Asia. The Gulf of Aqaba and the Suez Canal surround the peninsula. Israel, Sudan, and Libya are Egypt's land boundaries. The Mediterranean Sea and the Red Sea are water boundaries. Egypt is a little larger than Texas and New Mexico combined. The Western Desert, or Libyan Desert, covers two-thirds of the country. The Eastern Desert, or Arabian Desert, covers one-fourth of Egypt. The Nile, the world's longest river, flows from south to north between the two deserts. The Nile valley runs along the river. The Nile splits into streams to form the Nile delta. The rich valley and delta regions make up only 5 percent of the land, yet that is where most Egyptians live.

1

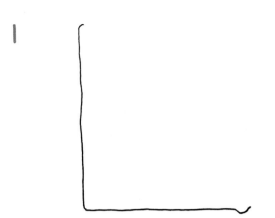

Begin your map of Egypt with a large *L*. Notice that it has little curves on the ends.

2

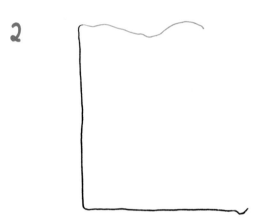

For the top boundary draw a wavy line.

3

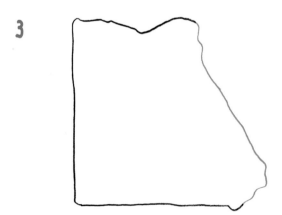

Draw a wavy diagonal line along the right side to show Egypt's Red Sea border.

4

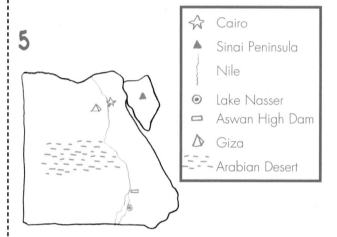

Draw a three-sided shape for the Sinai Peninsula. Notice the pointed bottom.

5

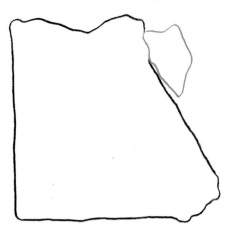

☆ Cairo

▲ Sinai Peninsula

ꟾ Nile

◉ Lake Nasser

▭ Aswan High Dam

△ Giza

- - - Arabian Desert

Create a legend box. Using the symbols shown, fill in Egypt's attractions.

a. Draw a star for Cairo.
b. Draw a triangle for the Sinai Peninsula.
c. Draw a vertical wavy line for the Nile.
d. Draw a circle with a dot inside for Lake Nasser.
e. Draw a rectangle for the Aswan High Dam.
f. Draw a pyramid for Giza.
g. Draw dashes for the Arabian Desert.

Flag of Egypt

Ancient Egyptians may have been the world's first flag makers. They mounted certain symbols on the tops of long poles. The symbols represented different parts of the kingdom. Thousands of years later, in 1923, Egypt established its first national flag. The current flag wasn't created until 1984. The flag features three horizontal stripes of red, white, and black. Red represents the 1952 struggle against British occupation. White stands for how the revolution was won without a war. Black represents the end of Egypt's troubles with the monarchy and British rule. Some say the white represents a bright future, and the black represents a dark past.

In the center of the white band is the national emblem. It is also the crest of Saladdin. He ruled Egypt and Syria in the twelfth century. The crest features a shield with an eagle. The eagle replaced the hawk, an earlier symbol. The hawk was connected with Muhammad, the founder of Islam. "Arab Republic of Egypt" is written in Arabic on a ribbon clutched in the eagle's claws.

1

Begin the Egyptian flag by drawing a rectangle. Add a horizontal line above the middle to make the top stripe.

2
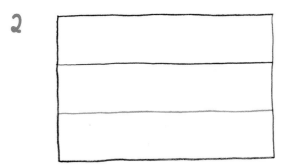

Add another horizontal line below the middle. You now have three stripes that are equal in size.

3
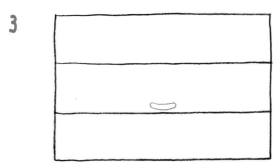

On the middle stripe start the eagle emblem with the small curved shape that contains the country's official name.

4

Add the eagle's feathered legs by drawing curved and straight lines. Draw its hooked feet above the curved ribbon.

5
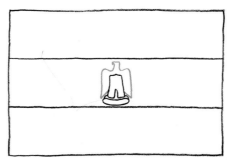

Draw a curved outline in the shape of an eagle's head and wings. Notice how the wings come to points at the ends.

6
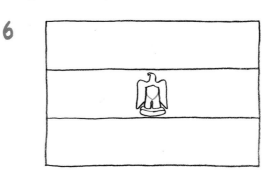

Draw a *U*-shaped line to form the shield in the center of the eagle's chest.

7

Add feathers to the wings using thin vertical lines. Color wide bars on the shield.

8
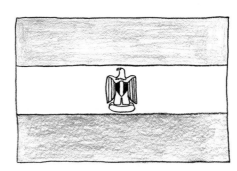

Shade the top and bottom stripes of the flag.

Camel

The Arabian camel has been an important animal to the Egyptians for centuries. People ride camels and use them to carry heavy loads. Bactrian camels have two humps. Arabian camels have only one. They have longer legs, less weight, and a shorter wool coat than do Bactrian camels. The Arabian camel stands about 7 feet (2.1m) tall at the shoulder. It can run at speeds of 8 to 10 miles per hour (12.9–16.1 km/h) for 18 hours. Its wide hooves step easily on desert sand.

Camels are not picky eaters. They eat whatever dried grasses, thorny plants, and shrubs they can find in the desert. When food is plentiful, the food a camel eats is stored as fat in its hump. When needed, the fat serves as both food and water. That is why camels can live for 17 days without eating or drinking.

1

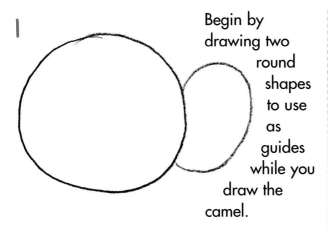

Begin by drawing two round shapes to use as guides while you draw the camel.

2

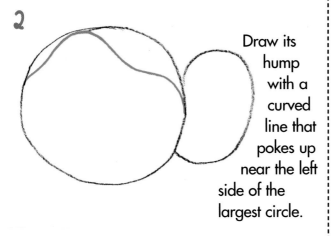

Draw its hump with a curved line that pokes up near the left side of the largest circle.

3

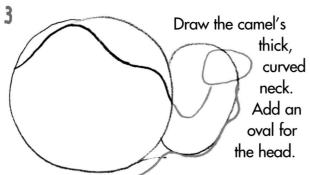

Draw the camel's thick, curved neck. Add an oval for the head.

4

Draw two little C-shaped ears, half circles for the nose, and a teardrop shape for the open mouth. Add a narrow, almond-shaped eye and a curved line for the chin.

5

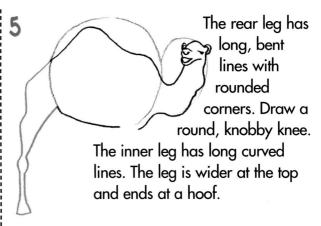

The rear leg has long, bent lines with rounded corners. Draw a round, knobby knee. The inner leg has long curved lines. The leg is wider at the top and ends at a hoof.

6

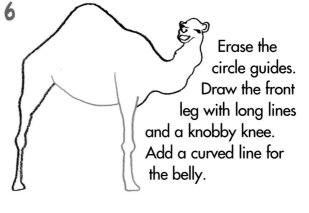

Erase the circle guides. Draw the front leg with long lines and a knobby knee. Add a curved line for the belly.

7

Add the rear legs in the same style used to draw the other legs.

8

Add shading to your camel. Use wavy squiggles to make the camel look furry.

19

Date Palm

Dates are the most common fruit in Egypt. They grow on trees called date palms. The trees grow to be about 75 feet (22.9 m) tall. Their leaves are used to provide

shade for other crops, such as cabbage. The tree trunks provide timber. When the leaves are dried, Egyptians weave them into crates and baskets.

Since the beginning of Egypt's history, dates have been a regular source of food. Today Egypt is the world's top producer of dates. The date, which has one seed, grows in bunches of dates weighing up to 18 pounds (8.2 kg). The fruit's size, shape, and color vary depending on how it grows. Dates are either eaten fresh or spread on the ground to dry. The date's juice, along with the tree's sap, is used to make syrup, drinks, and vinegar.

1

Begin by drawing a long shape that gets thinner toward the top. This will be the trunk of the date palm.

2

Add a lot of lines coming from the top of the trunk. These are the branches of the tree.

3

Draw curved diagonal lines on the trunk to make the bumpy, scaly look of the date palm bark.

4

Add the leaves of the palm by drawing many small diagonal lines on each branch.

5

Be sure to fill in the leaves on all of the branches.

6

Shade the bark and create a darker area at the top of the trunk where the leaves are thickest.

Step Pyramid of Djoser

Ancient Egyptians believed that they went to another life after death. They wanted to preserve and protect their bodies for the next world, so burial places were very important, especially to royalty. Early rulers were buried in sand pits and were covered with flat lids of mud. During King Djoser's reign in 2686 B.C., Imhotep, his master builder, created a pyramid for Djoser's burial site, in which to hide his gold and other treasures. Its square base and four sides that slope upward symbolized the king's rise to the heavens.

About 1 million tons (907,184.7 t) of stone were used to build the pyramid at Saqqara, near Cairo. It is called the Step Pyramid because its sides look like six stair steps. Egyptian kings that ruled after King Djoser were buried in pyramids that had smooth sides.

1

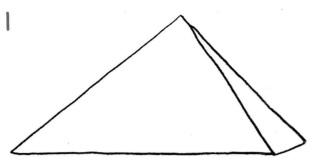

Begin the pyramid by drawing a triangle. Make the left side a bit longer than the right. Draw a thin triangle on the right side.

2

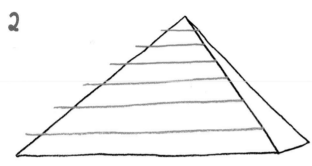

Draw a series of horizontal lines that extend beyond the left side of the pyramid.

3

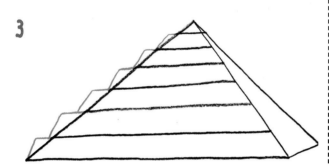

Connect each extended line with a short, slanted line to form a step.

4

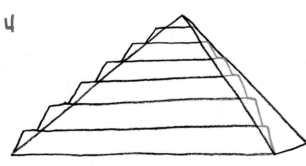

Next, create steps on the right side of the pyramid using the same short, curved vertical lines that you used on the left side.

5

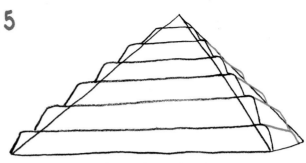

Create steps along the side of the pyramid with short horizontal lines.

6

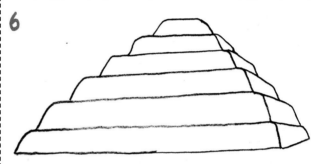

Erase the extra lines, including the pointed triangle at the top of the pyramid.

7

Shade the pyramid to make it look ancient. The right side should be shaded darker.

23

Mask of King Tut

Imagine being king of Egypt when you are only nine years old! Tutankhamen, or King Tut, was about that age when he took the throne around 1333 B.C. His reign lasted for only 10 years before he died. The cause of his death is not known. In 1922, English archaeologist Howard Carter found King Tut's tomb, or grave, in Egypt's Valley of the Kings. King Tut's small tomb was a great discovery because it was filled with thousands of treasures.

Ancient Egyptians believed in life after death. Over the face of King Tut's mummy was a mask that was created to help his spirit recognize him in his next life. The mask weighs more than 22 pounds (10 kg), and it is solid gold. It is decorated with colorful glass and precious stones. Tut's striped headcloth and wide collar were worn by royalty. The mask also shows him with a false beard. The vulture and the cobra on the mask are Egyptian symbols of protection.

24

1

Begin sketching King Tut's mask by sketching a long, vertical line. Then add two horizontal lines, as shown, to serve as guides as you draw King Tut's face.

2

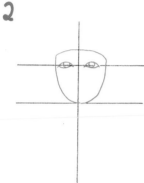

Draw a large *U* shape, as shown. Top it with a short line for his brow. Add two almond-shaped eyes with pupils inside.

3

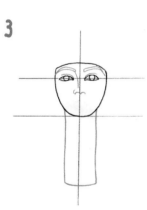

For his eyebrows, draw two narrow curved shapes, each coming to a point. Add curved lines for his eyelids, a curved vertical line for the nose, and curved lines for the nostrils. Add a long rectangular shape, which will be his neck and his chest.

4

Draw two large curved shapes for Tut's ears. Add small curved lines inside. Draw an *M* shape for the top lip. Draw a curved lower lip. Draw four lines around his neck.

5

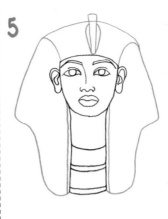

For Tut's headdress, draw long, curved lines from the top of each ear to the bottom of the neck. Add the crown shape above his head. Draw an ornament on top of his head.

6

Add a winding snake shape to the ornament. Draw a large *U* shape from one side of the headdress to the other.

7

Next add many thin, decorative lines to add a fancy look to King Tut's headdress.

8

Shade your drawing. Notice the shading on the eyes, necklace and headdress. Draw shadows on his cheeks to give depth to his cheekbones.

Egyptian Scarab

Ancient Egyptians, whether rich or poor, wore jewelry called amulets. Egyptians believed the amulets were good-luck charms. Amulets were supposed to protect people from evil. Amulets were thought to bring good things in this life and in the next life.

The most popular amulet was the scarab. It was named for a type of beetle and represented the Sun God Khepri. The real scarab beetle pushes a ball of its eggs covered in dung across the ground. Khepri was thought to roll the Sun across Earth in the same way. Scarabs often held simple messages, such as a wish or a prayer. Scarabs were usually carved from a precious stone and were painted blue or green. They were placed on bracelets and necklaces and were used on clay seals for important papers. The scarab was a symbol of endless life.

1

Begin by drawing a large heart. Add a small circle at the top.

2

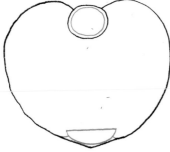

Erase the lines inside the circle. Add a second circle inside the first. Then draw a bowl shape at the bottom. Connect the bowl to the outside shape.

3

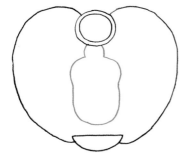

Erase the bottom point of the heart shape. Add the outline of a beetle's body, using curved lines, as shown.

4

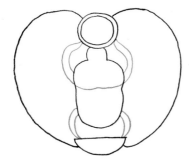

Divide the beetle's body into two sections with two curved lines in the center. Add four curved legs.

5

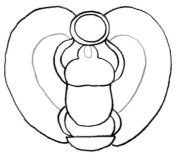

Draw two curved lines inside each half of the heart. Add a tiny oval at the top of the beetle to show the beetle's pincers.

6

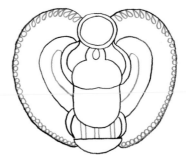

Draw two curved lines inside the smaller heart. Add six vertical lines below the beetle. Draw tiny teardrops and circles inside the large heart's border.

7

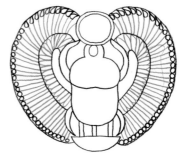

Decorate the scarab using curved lines. Repeat the lines until the two heart-shaped spaces are filled.

8

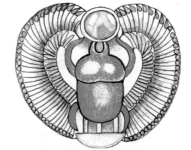

Shade your scarab. Keep white highlights on the jewel above the beetle.

27

Queen Nefertiti

Nefertiti was queen of Egypt from 1353 to 1341 B.C., when she was married to Pharaoh Akhenaton, also known as Amenhotep IV. They worshiped a new Sun God called Aton or Aten. This marked the first time that Egyptian religion accepted one god rather than many gods. In Nefertiti's time, Egyptian artists began to create sculptures and paintings that were lifelike.

Queen Nefertiti's name means "the beautiful woman has come." Was she beautiful? A sculptor named Thutmose seemed to think so. His famous bust, or sculpture, of Nefertiti was made in 1350 B.C. He carved the sculpture from a rock called limestone. Then he painted it with bold colors. The face is yellow-brown, like skin. The lips are red. The eyelids and eyebrows are outlined in black. Her necklace and royal crown are colorful, too. The left eye was unfinished, and, over time, the left ear was broken. Still, the sculpture offers a beautiful image of Queen Nefertiti.

1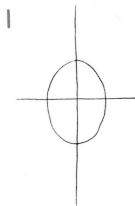

Draw an oval for Nefertiti's head. Draw a vertical and a horizontal line that cross in the center of the oval.

2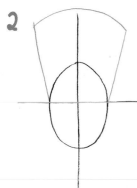

From the oval draw Nefertiti's crown using two long lines that are connected by a curved horizontal line, or arc, on top.

3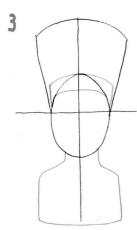

Add a band across Nefertiti's forehead using two curved lines and two small vertical lines. Draw the neck, shoulders, and chest using curved lines, as shown.

4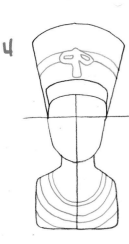

Add a band that wraps around her crown. In the center, draw the soft, curving lines that decorate the band. Add five U-shaped lines that will become her necklace.

5

Draw narrow shapes for Nefertiti's eyebrows and curved lines for her top eyelids. Notice that her eyebrows are extended to thin points.

6

Next draw Nefertiti's almond-shaped eyes, as shown. Extend the outer lashes beyond her eyes.

7

Darken her eyes to show her makeup. Add a small, wavy line for her nose. Draw her ears. Draw her full lips with a small M shape and two curved lines. Add small vertical lines and small circles in the bands on the crown and in the necklace.

8

Shade your drawing. Notice the darker shadows under her lip and on her chin and neck.

Temple of Ramses II

Ramses II, the greatest of Egypt's pharaohs, ruled for 66 years beginning in 1279 B.C. He was best remembered for what he left behind. He had at least 90 children. He also left more monuments to himself than did any other pharaoh.

His grandest monument was the Great Temple at Abu Simbel in southern Egypt. It was built into a cliff along the Nile River. At the entrance to the temple, four statues of Ramses II are carved into the rock. The statues are each 67 feet (20.4 m) tall. They show Ramses II wearing the double crown of Upper and Lower Egypt. The temple was built to let sunlight reach 160 feet (48.8 m) inside the temple to shine on the statues on two days each year, Ramses's birthday and the day he was crowned king! When the Aswan High Dam was built in the 1960s, Lake Nasser's rising waters would have flooded the temple. Builders moved the temple to higher ground between 1963 and 1969.

1

Draw a long vertical line to use as a guide as you draw one of the figures at the entrance of the tomb. Begin at the top of the figure by drawing a triangle for his hat.

2

Add a *U* for the figure's head and two vertical lines for his neck.

3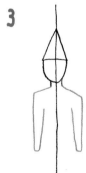

Add two straight arms. The ancient Egyptian style for sculpting a figure was to make it look strong and stiff. Over time, the hands have been worn away.

4

Add the lower part of the body using vertical lines that curve a bit at the waist and hips. Notice the way the leg on the right comes forward as though he is taking a step.

5

Erase extra lines. Add the band to the hat. Put a *U* in the center of the band. Draw the curve of his hat inside the triangle guide line, as shown.

6

Erase extra lines. Add a long rectangle to the chin. Draw almond-shaped eyes and small lines for the nose and the mouth.

7

Add lines at the chest, a belly button and a line for the top of the figure's skirt. Draw a rectangular box around the figure. Let the foot come forward out of the box.

8

Shade your drawing. Notice the deep shadows behind the figure and at the top of the box.

Feluccas

   Boats have sailed on the Nile River for thousands of years. In addition to using the boats for travel, ancient Egyptians used their boats to move huge stones down the river for building pyramids. They carried mummies to their burial ground by boat. Then they buried models of their boats in the tombs for the dead pharaoh's use in the next life.

   Modern Egyptians love to sail feluccas on the Nile River and the Mediterranean Sea. A felucca is a narrow sailing boat that speeds along by using the power of the wind. It has one sail, shaped like a sloping triangle. The sail is usually longer than the boat itself. A rudder is used to steer the boat. Before the rudder was invented in the mid-thirteenth century, oars and paddles were used to steer boats. Feluccas are small and not very comfortable. They give people a special view of Egyptian life, though, especially along the Nile River.

1

Draw two long horizontal lines. Make the top line curve up at the left side. Add a line at each end to make the shape a box.

2

Draw the other side of the boat with a long line and connect in the front as shown.

3

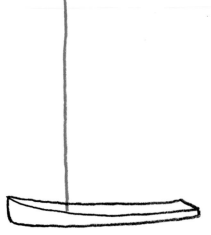

Draw a vertical line to hold the sail.

4

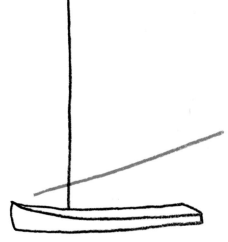

Add a diagonal line.

5

Draw two more lines to complete the sail. The sides of the triangle should be curved.

6

Add two lines that attach the sail to the boat.

7

Add another line along the side of the boat. Draw water beneath the boat. Add an outline inside the sail shape.

8

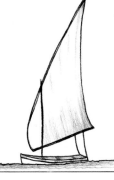

Add the little benches inside the boat. Shade the drawing.

Cleopatra

Egyptians have always loved their queen Cleopatra. She was the only member of her Greek-born ruling family to speak their language.

Cleopatra is shown here in a kind of sculpture called a bas-relief. A bas-relief is a sculpture in which the background has been cut away. Above the figure of Cleopatra is her cartouche. A cartouche is usually an oval-shaped frame that is wrapped around a picture and characters called hieroglyphs. Around 3000 B.C., Egyptians wrote in hieroglyphics, a system of writing that uses pictures of people, birds, rabbits, lions, human eyes, and other shapes and symbols. Egyptian royalty placed their names within the cartouches. Cartouches often appeared on ancient Egyptian monuments, temples, and mummy cases, or coffins. In a hieroglyphic, the animals and the people always face toward the beginning of the line.

1

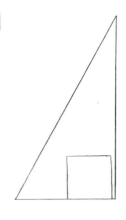

In this drawing, Cleopatra's body will fit into a triangle. Draw a triangle to use as a guide as you draw her. Draw a square for her seat.

2

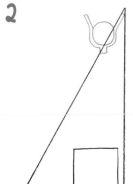

At the top of the triangle, draw a circle inside the shape shown.

3

Look carefully at the shape of her headdress and hair. Notice that the front of her headdress is shaped like a bird's head with a beak. The wing drops down the side of her head. Using a series of straight and curved lines, draw the shape of the headdress and hair.

4

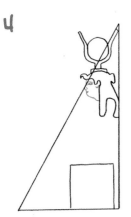

Draw an arc for her forehead. Follow the slant of the triangle for her nose. Add a curved line for her chin. Add another curve for the ear. Draw an almond-shaped eye and an arc for the eyebrow.

5

Draw long, softly curved lines for her arms. Each arm is slightly bent into a backward *L* shape. The fingers are made using long, tiny ovals. Add a vertical line for her chest.

6

Draw her leg using long, bent lines. Notice that the line becomes horizontal at the foot. Add an arc for Cleopatra's lower back.

7

Erase the triangle guide. Add her staff by drawing vertical lines and adding a tiny circle to the bottom. Add a thin diamond shape to the top. Draw the ankh symbol in her other hand. It looks like a cross with a rounded loop on one end.

8

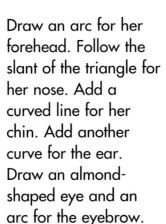

Add details to her hair by drawing wavy lines. Draw detail to the bird's face on the headdress. Draw a line across her chest. Shade the areas, as shown, to finish your drawing.

Muhammad Ali Mosque

Mosques are everywhere in Cairo, Egypt's capital. They are temples where Muslims practice the faith of Islam. One of the best-known is the Muhammad Ali Mosque. It is also known as the Alabaster Mosque because its walls are made of a white mineral called alabaster. It overlooks the city from atop the Citadel. The Citadel was a fortress begun in 1176, from which Egypt was ruled for 700 years. Completed in 1857, the mosque is named for Muhammad Ali, an army officer from Turkey. He became pasha, or governor, of Egypt in 1805. He developed Egypt into a modern country by creating new jobs and building new schools. The stone mosque has giant silver domes on the roofs and two 270-foot-tall (82.3-m-tall) minarets, or towers. Muhammad Ali is buried in the courtyard.

1 Draw the two large main shapes of the front of the mosque with a large rectangle and a rectangular box in front.

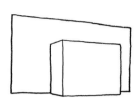

2 Draw two arcs and a larger arc, which is the dome, on top. Add a small rectangular tower. Add a dome and a line on top of the tower. Add three vertical lines under the arch in the left.

3 Behind the large rectangle, add four rectangles, for the side of the mosque, that slant backward into the distance. Add small arcs on these buildings.

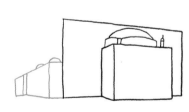

4 Draw a wall on the left side of the building. Draw two tall towers at the corners of the front rectangle. Add three large domes above the front of the mosque.

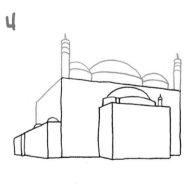

5 Draw an even larger dome on top of the others. Add two more towers and connect them to the dome with straight lines. Draw small lines from the towers and domes.

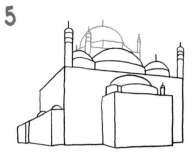

6 Draw the two tall towers with triangular tops at the rear of the mosque. Draw triangular and arched roofs above the left wall.

7 Draw many rectangular and arched windows. Add an arched entryway on the lower left. Behind that draw vertical lines for columns.

8 Add shading to your drawing.

Minarets

Arabian Muslims have changed the look of Egypt by adding many Islamic buildings. Mosques are especially important because they are the places where Muslims pray and worship. Churches are topped by  steeples, but mosques have tall, thin towers called minarets. Near the top of the minaret is a balcony where, five times daily, an officer of the mosque, known as a muezzin, calls people to pray. Today the muezzin's call is made through loudspeakers. It is also heard on the radio and on television.

The earliest minarets were short with square bottoms and rounded caps at the top. Later minarets became tall and slender structures with fancy decorations. A third type was created by Turkish Muslims. This style is long and slender and shaped like a pencil, with simple wooden railings and little decoration. The sixteenth-century minarets of the Mosque of Suleiman Pasha in Cairo were built in this style.

1

Draw the base, or bottom, of the minaret with diagonal and vertical lines.

2

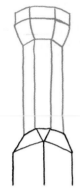

Add on the next level of the minaret with long vertical lines. On top of this long section, draw four more vertical lines. Add a top section with four more vertical lines and a horizontal line.

3

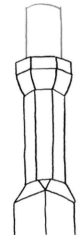

Draw a cylinder. A cylinder is made by drawing two vertical lines and one curved line on top.

4

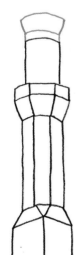

Draw a bowl-shaped section with a base on top of the cylinder.

5

Draw a ring on top of this level. Top that with two curved, vertical lines. Add a small horizontal shape. Next draw a ball on the top.

6

Begin adding the decorative details. You can create these by drawing tiny arches, lines, and circles. Add a vertical line to the top of the ball.

7

Continue adding the decorative details to the lower section, including the long archways on the lower level.

8

Add shading to show the design of the minaret.

Islamic Tile

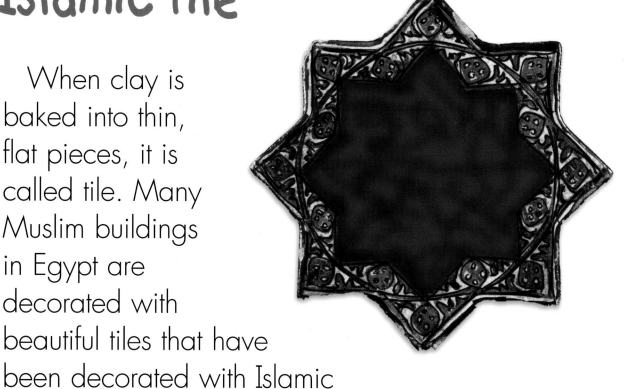

When clay is baked into thin, flat pieces, it is called tile. Many Muslim buildings in Egypt are decorated with beautiful tiles that have been decorated with Islamic designs. Islamic tile work is a craft that started about 800 years ago. All Islamic art is based on the Muslim belief that Muhammad is the holy messenger of Allah, or God. In the seventh century, Muhammad preached against the worship of any other god. Islamic law forbids Muslims from representing human or animal forms in art. Instead Muslim artists make patterns. They may be either from the Arabic alphabet or swirling lines and patterns called arabesques. Shapes such as circles, triangles, and hexagons, which have six sides, are also used. These tiles may cover an entire wall, floor, or roof.

40

1

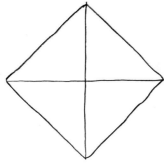

The beautiful shape and design of the tile is made by layering squares, diamonds, circles, and ovals. First draw a diamond shape. Draw two lines to divide it into four equal parts.

2

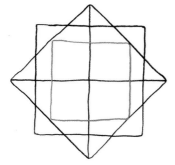

Next draw a square on top of the diamond.

3

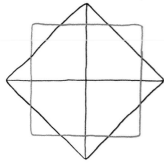

Add a smaller square inside the larger square.

4

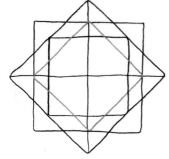

Next draw another diamond inside the first diamond.

5

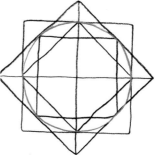

Draw a circle inside the largest square.

6

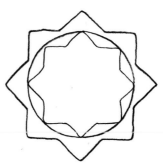

Erase the lines of the squares and diamonds that you don't need. You are left with two eight-pointed stars and a circle.

7

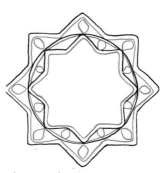

Draw a second line inside each of the shapes to make double lines. Add loops inside each of the shapes for decorations.

8

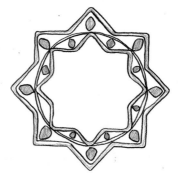

Shade your drawing. If you like, you can add more designs in the center of the tile.

Aswan High Dam

Before Egypt built dams, banks along the Nile River flooded. The floods brought rich silt, or earth, to the Nile valley. Farmers planted crops after a flood.

Egypt completed its first dam in 1902 at Aswan to help control the floodwaters so that farmers could plant and protect their crops year-round. As Egypt's population grew, it needed more water and more hydroelectric power. The Aswan High Dam was built to meet these needs.

Completed in 1970, the dam took 10 years to build, at the enormous cost of one billion dollars. It is one of the world's largest structures, extending more than 2 miles (3.2 km) across the Nile River. It also created Lake Nassar, the world's largest human-made lake. The lake stores water that is used for farmland.

1

First use a jagged line to draw the land next to the dam. Then add the gateway to the dam by drawing straight lines as shown.

2

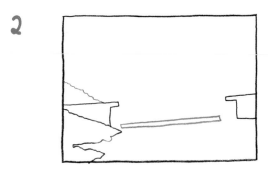

Draw a long, thin rectangle between the gate. Add another hill above the gate at the left.

3

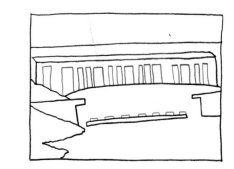

Draw a gentle curve across your picture area.

4

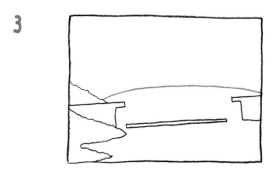

Begin the dam with two long horizontal lines and four short vertical lines.

5

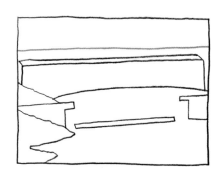

Draw a line above the dam. This is a road that stretches above the water.

6

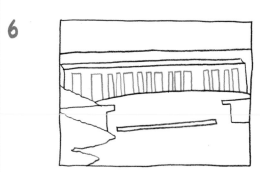

Fill the front of the dam with long rectangles.

7

Draw small shapes on the long, thin bar at the front of the dam.

8

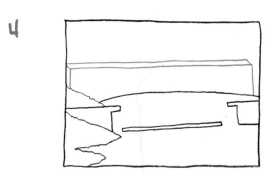

Shade your drawing. Draw short lines to make the land look rough and rocky. Add shadows inside the dam, and shade the water with smooth lines.

43

Timeline

3100 B.C.	Menes unites the kingdoms of Upper Egypt and Lower Egypt. He becomes Egypt's first king.
2580 B.C.	The Great Pyramid at Giza is completed.
525 B.C.	Persians conquer Egypt. Egypt remains under foreign rule for 2,500 years.
1799	Scientists discover how to read hieroglyphics.
1805–1849	Muhammad Ali founds modern Egypt.
1869	The Suez Canal is completed.
1952	End of Egyptian monarchy and British rule.
1953	Egypt becomes a republic.
1967	Israel takes the Sinai Peninsula from Egypt in the Six-Day War.
1979	Egyptian president Anwar el-Sadat signs a peace treaty with Israel. The Sinai Peninsula is returned to Egypt.
1981	Anwar el-Sadat is murdered. Hosni Mubarak becomes Egypt's next president.

Egypt Fact List

Official Name	Arab Republic of Egypt
Area	386,662 square miles (1,001,450 sq km)
Continents	Africa; Sinai Peninsula is in Asia
Population	65,239,000
Capital	Cairo, population 6,789,000
Most Populated City	Cairo
Industries	Crude oil and petroleum products, textiles, food processing, tourism, and natural gas
Agriculture	Cotton, rice, corn, wheat, beans, and fruits
National Anthem	"Biladi" ("My Hometown")
Official Language	Arabic
Common Phrases	Ma' alesh, "it doesn't matter" or "don't take it seriously"; ahlan wa sahlan, "welcome"
Currency	Egyptian pound
National Holiday	July 23, Anniversary of the 1952 Revolution
Popular Sport	Soccer
Favorite Dish	Falafel, or fried balls of chickpeas and wheat
Longest River	Nile, 4,160 miles (6,694.9 km)
Major Lake	Lake Nasser, 312 square miles (808.1 sq km)
Highest Peak	Mount St. Catherine, 8,625 feet (2,628.9 m)
Major Religions	Islam, Coptic Christianity
Boundaries	Israel, Lybia, Sudan, the Mediterranean Sea, and the Red Sea

Glossary

archaeologist (ar-kee-AH luh-jist) Someone who studies the remains of peoples to understand how they lived.

bas-relief (bah-rih-LEEF) A raised carving.

bazaars (buh-ZARZ) Markets in the Middle East and Asia that consist of rows of small shops or stalls.

burial sites (BER-ee-ul SYTS) Places where bodies are buried.

cartouche (kar-TOOSH) A frame that surrounds Egyptian writing.

civilizations (sih-vih-lih-ZAY-shunz) People living in an organized way.

delta (DEL-tuh) A pile of earth and sand that collects at the mouth of a river.

descended (dih-SEN-did) Born of a certain family or group.

design (dih-ZYN) A decorative pattern.

dung (DUNG) Animal waste.

embassies (EM-buh-seez) Official homes or offices in a foreign country.

emblem (EM-blum) A picture with a saying on it.

exhibitions (ek-sih-BIH-shunz) Public shows.

faculty (FA-kul-tee) The teachers in a school or college.

horizontal (hor-ih-ZON-til) Level and flat.

human-made (HYOO-man-mayd) Made by people rather than nature.

hydroelectric (hy-droh-ih-LEK-trik) Having energy that is created by flowing water.

impressionist (im-PREH-shuh-nist) Having to do with an artist who paints in a style of art in which the subject is not as important as how the artist uses color and tone.

industry (IN-dus-tree) A moneymaking business in which many people work and make money producing a particular product.

mineral (MIH-ner-ul) A natural element that is not an animal, or a plant, or another living thing.

monarchy (MAH-nar-kee) A government run by a king or a queen.

monastery (MAH-nuh-ster-ee) A house where people who have taken religious vows live and work.

monks (MUNKS) Men who have made certain promises based on their beliefs and who live in a special house.

monuments (MON-yoo-mints) Objects made to honor a person or an event.

mummy (MUH-mee) A body prepared for burial in a certain way that makes it last a long time.

oases (oh-AY-seez) Areas in a desert where plants can grow because of a water source.

occupation (ah-kyoo-PAY-shun) The kind of work a person does to earn a living.

peninsula (peh-NIN-suh-luh) An area of land that is surrounded by water on three sides.

prime minister (PRYM MIH-nih-ster) The leader of a government.

republic (ree-PUB-lik) A form of government in which the authority belongs to the people. The people in a republic have the power to elect representatives who manage the government.

resources (REE-sors-ez) A supply or source of energy or useful materials.

revolution (reh-vuh-LOO-shun) A complete change in government.

steeples (STEE-pulz) Church towers.

Stone Age (STOHN AYJ) A time when very early humans used tools and weapons made from stone.

survived (sur-VYVD) Stayed alive.

symbols (SIM-bulz) Objects or designs that stand for something else.

textile (TEK-styl) Woven fabric or cloth.

timber (TIM-bur) Wood that is cut and used for building houses, ships, and other wooden objects.

Index

Web Sites

Due to the changing nature of Internet links, PowerKids Press has developed an online list of Web sites related to the subject of this book. This site is updated regularly. Please use this link to access the list.
www.powerkidslinks.com/kgdc/egypt/